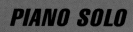

MARVEL
AVENGERS
AGE OF ULTRON

**MUSIC FROM THE
MOTION PICTURE SOUNDTRACK**

Images and artwork © 2015 MARVEL
MARVEL SUPERHEROES MUSIC

ISBN 978-1-4950-2953-0

DISTRIBUTED BY

HAL•LEONARD®
CORPORATION

7777 W. BLUEMOUND RD. P.O. BOX 13819 MILWAUKEE, WI 53213

In Australia Contact:
Hal Leonard Australia Pty. Ltd.
4 Lentara Court
Cheltenham, Victoria, 3192 Australia
Email: ausadmin@halleonard.com.au

Visit Hal Leonard Online at
www.halleonard.com

*Not featured in film.

HEROES

Music by
DANNY ELFMAN

Moderately fast

FARMHOUSE

Music by
DANNY ELFMAN

Moderately slow, expressively

Pedal ad lib. throughout

Slightly faster

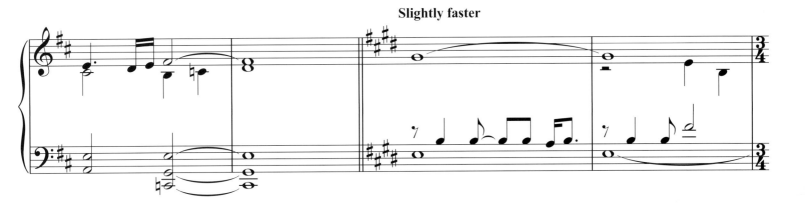

CAN YOU STOP THIS THING?

Music by
DANNY ELFMAN

THE MISSION

Music by
BRIAN TYLER

WISH YOU WERE HERE

Music by
BRIAN TYLER

Slowly, expressively

Pedal ad lib. throughout

Moderately, steadily

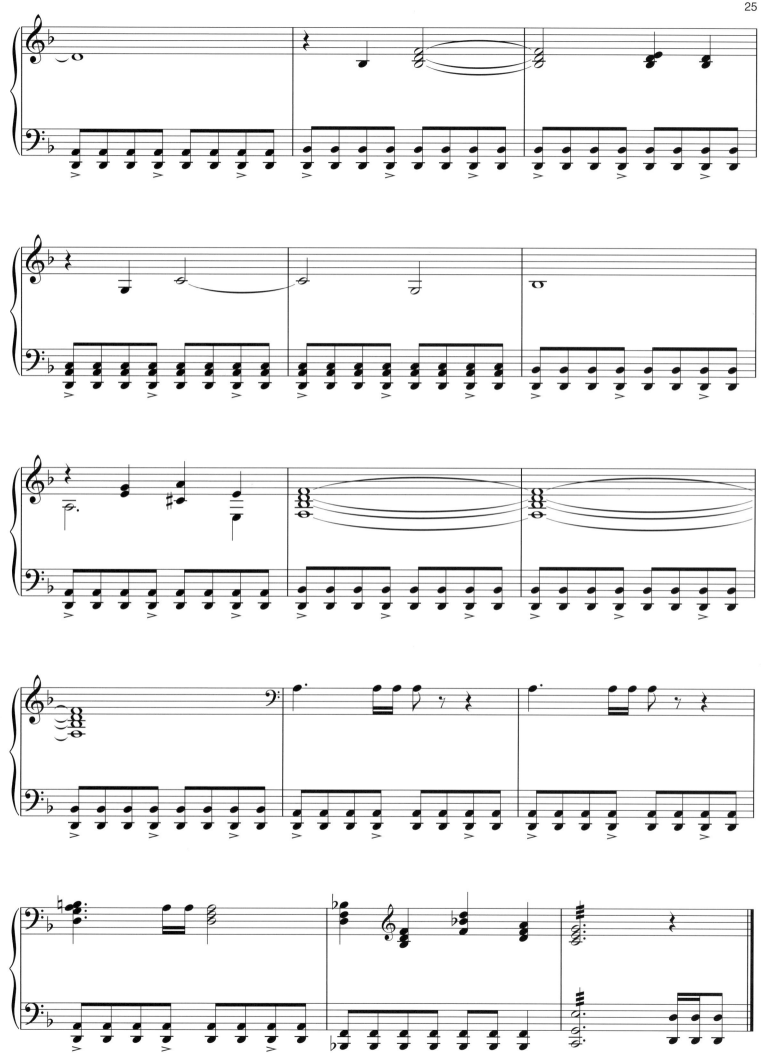

AVENGERS UNITE

Music by
DANNY ELFMAN

NOTHING LASTS FOREVER

Music by
DANNY ELFMAN